Celebrating *150 years* of Aberdeen's famous concert hall

Edi Swan

Published by Aberdeen Performing Arts and Aberdeen City Libraries 2009

Published by Aberdeen Performing Arts and Aberdeen City Libraries

Aberdeen Performing Arts
His Majesty's Theatre
Rosemount Viaduct
Aberdeen AB25 1GL
www.boxofficeaberdeen.com

ISBN - 978-0-9563261-0-2

Designed by Coleen Matheson, Aberdeen Performing Arts.

Printed by John Good Holbrook.

MUSIC HALL

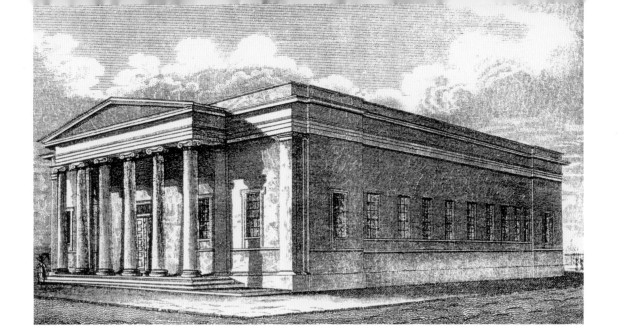

Music Hall

In 1993, Jim Pratt, Senior Librarian at Aberdeen Central Library, researched and wrote an excellent short history entitled The Music Hall. This was reprinted in full colour in 2008 as a preliminary taster for the Sesquicentennial Celebrations in September 2009.

My commission from Aberdeen Performing Arts was to augment that publication with extra stories and illustrations to highlight the multi-functional use of The Music Hall large concert hall. This was added, in 1859, to what was then called The County Assembly Rooms.

ELEVATION AND GROUND PLAN OF A SUITE OF PUBLIC ROOMS AT ABERDEEN,
For the accommodation of the Meetings of the conjoined Counties of
ABERDEEN, BANFF, KINCARDINE & FORFAR, 1820.

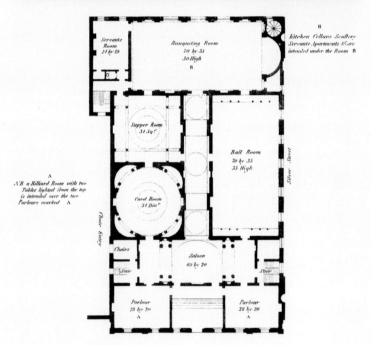

Archibald Simpson's original design for The County Assembly Rooms

The County Assembly Rooms

At the beginning of the 19th century, Aberdeen was growing in prosperity and developing as a commercial centre. However, no proper central meeting place or assembly rooms were accessible where polite society and the intelligentsia of the day could meet. The building of better roads had eased travel between county and city, and it is mainly due to the enthusiasm of the landed gentry that a suitable assembly room was eventually built.

There were meeting places in the city. The now long-gone New Inn at the corner of Castle Street and King Street had one of the earliest entertainment stages in the city. The Lemon Tree Tavern in Huxter Row, now buried under the Town House, was very popular during its 50-year ownership by the worthy Mrs Ronald. It is said that Burns and Johnson would have left the city with more favourable impressions had they partaken of the Lemon Tree Tavern's hospitality and had they been served by Mrs Ronald. However, it was lamented at the time 'assemblies are, of necessity, obliged to be held in taverns which are very incommodious and ill adapted to such a purpose'.

In 1807, a public meeting held in the Lemon Tree Tavern brought a promise of £500 towards the project. The next year, a gifted young architect, John Chisholm, produced a 'Design for the New Assembly Room for Aberdeen', which was of such importance and originality that it was exhibited at the prestigious Royal Academy in London although nothing came of it then. A second abortive attempt was made in 1815, the year of Waterloo. Interest was growing and a third attempt in 1818 at the Annual Race Meeting at the Aberdeen Links brought, at last, a positive result. By the end of the year, subscriptions had reached the £7,000 mark. The published list of subscribers reveals the support of the landed gentry with substantial contributions from the Duke of Gordon, the Earl of Aberdeen, the Marquis of Huntly and residents of Echt, Pitfoddels, Drumtochtie, Pitfour, Rannes and Clova to name but a few. Indeed, without the support from '12 mile roon', the competition for the design of the new Assembly Rooms might never have been launched.

LIST OF SUBSCRIBERS		
TO		
THE NEW PUBLIC ROOMS.		
Town of Aberdeen — —	—	L.900
His Grace the Duke of Gordon	—	100
The Right Honble. the Earl of Aberdeen		100
The Most Noble the Marquis of Huntly		50
5 Provost Brebner — —	—	100
Duncan Davidson, advocate	—	100
Alexr. Fraser, merchant	—	100
William Forbes of Echt —	—	100
James Farquhar of London	—	100
10 Hugh Gordon of Madras	—	100
John Garioch, merchant —		100
James Hadden, do. —	—	100
George Hogarth, do. —	—	100
George Hogarth, jun. do.	—	100
15 William Kennedy, advocate	—	100
Patrick Kilgour of Woodside		100
Thomas Leys of Glasgowforest	—	100
John Menzies of Pitfoddels		100
Alexr. Pirie, merchant	—	100
20 William Pirie, do. —	—	100
John Amand, do. —	—	50
John Anderson of Calcutta	—	50
Charles Bannerman, advocate		50
Thomas Black, merchant —	—	50
25 John Blackie, plumber —	—	50
James Brebner, merchant		50
Thomas Burnett, advocate —	—	50
William Carnegie, do. —	—	50
John Catto, merchant —	—	50

An advertisement in the local press brought a response of ten designs from distinguished architects across the country. Three were thought to be worthy of further consideration. The first prize of 50 guineas went to a local man, Archibald Simpson. Although he had designed and built some very fine buildings in the city and the shire, he chose to enter the competition under an assumed name. The completion of The County Assembly Rooms established his position as one of Aberdeen's leading architects.

The Foundation Stone

On Wednesday, 26th April, 1820, a huge assembly gathered at the Castlegate. Despite heavy rain the parade set off at 2pm. Led by a party of soldiers from the 80th Regiment who were to clear a way through the gathering crowd of spectators, some 1500 brethren, from the Lodges of Freemasons in the city and the neighbourhood, wearing the emblems of their office and carrying their regalia, marched up Union Street to the site of the new Assembly Rooms. Legend has it that Archibald Simpson led the parade waving his set of plans aloft. At the site, the foundation stone, containing five coins of the realm, was 'founded with full Masonic honors by James, Earl of Fife, Depute Grand Master of Scotland, First Year of the Reign of George The Fourth'. The rooms were duly completed in 1822 at a cost of about £11,500, and the plans showed a suite of rooms consisting of a banqueting hall, a ballroom, a supper room, a card room and two parlours on the ground floor. On the floor above were two billiard rooms and the hall-keeper's apartments. The cellars and kitchen were in the basement.

Archibald Simpson

ABERDEEN PUBLIC ROOMS

Built by subscription

FOUNDED WITH MASONIC HONORS

BY JAMES, EARL OF FIFE

**DEPUTE GRAND MASTER FOR SCOTLAND
APRIL 26, 1820**

FIRST YEAR OF THE REIGN OF GEORGE THE FOURTH

ARCHD. SIMPSON, ARCHITECT

*Facsimile of engraved plate
on the foundation stone*

Famous Names

For the next 36 years, the Assembly Rooms served their original purpose without actually making any profit. Indeed, the majority of the subscribers did not expect any return. There were occasions when the building was packed to overflowing. Visits by Charles Stratton, better known as General Tom Thumb; Mystic Temple with John Anderson, The Great Wizard of the North and readings by Charles Dickens proved very popular.

Many other top-quality artistes were unwilling to make the journey north as there was not a hall within the County Assembly Rooms to meet their needs. Much bitterness was voiced that Aberdonians were denied the privilege of seeing and hearing the famous 'Swedish Nightingale' Jenny Lind.

Charles Dickens

Miss Jenny Lind, The Swedish Nightingale, who 'came, sang and conquered' at her appearance in The Music Hall in 1861

John Henry Anderson

> **COUNTY ROOMS, ABERDEEN.**
>
> ON Monday Night, the GREAT WIZARD of the NORTH'S MYSTIC TEMPLE was opened, and crowded by a most Brilliant Audience—the *Elite* of the City. Hundreds were turned from the Doors, who could not gain admission! Never was an audience more delighted—all were astonished, as wonder followed wonder! Some were heard to say—
> "IS HE MORTAL?" "CAN SUCH THINGS BE?"
> This is the best proof of the wonderful and truly magnificent nature of the
> **GREAT WIZARD OF THE NORTH'S**
> UNPARALLELED FEATS,
> Which are now the general theme of wonder and conversation in all circles of society.
>
> On this and every Evening during the Week,
> **THE GREAT WIZARD OF THE NORTH,**
> Will appear in his
> MYSTIC LABORATORY,
> And perform all his
> NEW MIRACLES
> And seemingly
> **Superhuman Wonders of Natural Magic!**
> Which were performed by him before the Queen, Prince Albert, and Court, at Buckingham Palace.
>
> Reserved Seats, 2s. 6d.; Second Seats, 2s.; Back Seats, 1s.; Gallery, 6d.
> Doors open at half-past 7—commence at 8 o'clock.
>
> *REMEMBER HIS STAY IS SHORT—DELAY NOT!*

150 years

County Rooms, Aberdeen.

POSITIVELY FOR FIVE DAYS ONLY:

Tuesday, Wednesday, Thursday, Friday, and Saturday,

3d, 4th, 5th, 6th, and 7th February, as he appears in Brechin on Monday.

FAREWELL LEVEES

OF

GENERAL

TOM THUMB,

Previous to his final departure to America.

Under the Patronage of HER MAJESTY, PRINCE ALBERT, the QUEEN DOWAGER, the KING and QUEEN of the FRENCH, the KING and QUEEN of the BELGIANS, the EMPEROR of RUSSIA, the QUEENS of SPAIN, the Royal Families and Nobility of England, France, Belgium, and Spain, and *visited by more than 2,000,000 persons* during last 2 years.

The Little General is in fine health and spirits, Symmetrical in his Proportions, and has NOT INCREASED AN INCH IN HEIGHT, nor AN OUNCE IN WEIGHT, SINCE HE WAS SEVEN MONTHS OLD! *He is Fourteen Years of Age, Twenty-five Inches High, and Weighs only Fifteen Pounds!!!*

The Little General will appear in his various Extraordinary Performances and Costumes, including SONGS, DANCES, ANCIENT STATUES, IMITATIONS of NAPOLEON and FREDERICK THE GREAT, **Highland Costume**, CITIZEN'S DRESS, and the unique and elegant **New French Court Dress**, worn before the King, Queen, and Royal Family at the Tuilleries and Palace of St. Cloud. The MAGNIFICENT PRESENTS received from the First Crowned Heads in the world will be exhibited. **The General's Miniature Equipage will Promenade the Streets daily.**

Hours of Exhibition: 11½ to 1; 2½ to 4; and from 7 to 8½; except on TUESDAY, when the Hours will be from 3½ to 5, and 7 to 8½. Doors open Half an Hour previous.

Admission, One Shilling. Children under Ten, Half-price.

In order to accommodate the WORKING CLASSES, the Price to the THIRD LEVEE will be reduced to each person SIXPENCE, except to Reserved Places, the Price to which will be same as at the Morning Levees.

G. CORNWALL, PRINTER, ABERDEEN.

The New Music Hall

In 1858, the rooms were sold by the trustees to the newly formed Aberdeen Music Hall Company, which swiftly produced plans to extend the building to accommodate a grand Music Hall with a seating capacity of 2500. This was to be achieved by demolishing the existing dining room and extending out into what is now Golden Square. It would be enhanced by a stage area large enough to take a full orchestra and chorus, placed in front of a new organ commissioned from Mr Henry Willis of London. The link with the original architect was continued with the acceptance of the design for the new Music Hall by Mr James Matthews, who received his early training at Archibald Simpson's practice.

After five years further training in the London practice of the noted architect Sir George Gilbert Scott, James Matthews returned to Aberdeen to enter into practice with Thomas Mackenzie. Later in 1877, Matthews joined with Thomas Mackenzie's son, A. Marshall Mackenzie, to form Matthews and Mackenzie. The two architects were responsible for many distinguished buildings in the city. These included The New Grammar School, The Town and County Bank, The Free Church College, St John's Episcopal Church, most of Rubislaw Terrace, The Free South Church, The Art Gallery, The Harbour Office and a number of mansion houses across the county. Matthews also played an import role in the erection of Her Majesty's Theatre and Opera House in Guild Street, now known as The Tivoli Theatre, where he was the supervising architect for the designs of the eminent theatre architect, Charles Phipps.

In 1883, after 18 years as a conscientious town councillor, Matthews was elected Lord Provost of Aberdeen to be the guiding hand over the City Improvements Bill, which opened up new access to Rosemount and numerous changes in Ferryhill and other parts of the city. In 1885, on the occasion of the opening of the Mitchell Hall and Tower, which was designed by his partner A. Marshall Mackenzie, Aberdeen University conferred on Matthews the honorary degree of LLD.

James Matthews

Plan of The Music Hall for a Japanese Bazaar in 1899, showing Matthews' design for the new concert hall

Her Majesty's Theatre and Opera House in Guild Street

A Royal Occasion

On 14th September, 1859, The Music Hall was ready for the arrival of Prince Albert, Prince Consort. He came down from Balmoral to inaugurate the British Association's Conference, of which he was president.

Later that month, the hall was the setting for the conferring of the Freedom of the City on Lord John Russell before an audience of some 2000. On that occasion, the now completed Henry Willis organ was played for the first time with Willis himself at the keyboard. The organ was originally built for the Crystal Palace, London Exhibition, in 1854 and was donated to the city thanks to the generosity of a Leeds businessman. It is reputed to be the best organ in Scotland.

Prince Albert, Prince Consort

Prior to the formation of The Aberdeen Music Hall Company and its subsequent purchase of the Assembly Rooms and the building of the new Music Hall, the council chambers had called for a hall that could accommodate musical entertainment of the highest calibre at ticket prices affordable by 'all Classes of the Community'. The spin off from this would be a venue that would accommodate large public meetings with audiences of around 2000 - 3000. The company subsequently bought the Assembly Rooms for £3000 and built and furnished The Music Hall for an additional £4500.

The opening of the British Association Conference in The Music Hall on 14th September 1859

The Aberdeen Choral Union

Musical recitals and entertainments became a regular feature of social life in the city with the Aberdeen Music Hall Choral Union, which had been formed earlier in 1859, playing a leading role. Their policy was to give four concerts per year - some sacred, some secular. The programmes would also include organ solos and pieces by the union's instrumental band.

December 31, 1892. BON-ACCORD. 7

Aberdeen Choral Union.
Conductor ... ... MR JOHN KIRBY.

ANNUAL PERFORMANCE
OF THE
"MESSIAH,"
IN THE
MUSIC HALL, on Tuesday, 3rd January, 1893.
Artistes:
MISS MEDORA HENSON, Soprano.
MISS MAUD BAKER, Contralto.
MR JOSEPH O'MARA, Tenor.
MR DAVID HUGHES, Bass.
CHORAL UNION AND BAND.
ORGANIST... ... ... MR G. C. DAWSON, F.C.O.
ADMISSION ... ... 3/-, 2/-, 1/6, and 1/- TICKETS from MUSICSELLERS.
Doors Open, 7 ; Commence, 7·45 ; Conclude, 10·15.

All members of the union - 82 trebles, 48 altos, 54 tenors and 62 basses - gave their services free of charge. Guest artistes, of course, were paid. Miss Helen Kirk, of Glasgow, became such a favourite that her fee was doubled and then trebled for each of her visits. Choral concerts became so popular that in 1870 a series of ten concerts were to feature 'a Choir of One Thousand Voices', singing psalms and hymn tunes. With the audience joining in the popular choruses, the effect must have been really special.

ON FRIDAY EVENING.
ABERDEEN CHORAL UNION.
LAST APPEARANCE OF MISS HELEN KIRK.
GRAND MISCELLANEOUS CONCERT,
IN
MUSIC HALL,
ON
FRIDAY, 9th MAY, 1862.
SOLOISTS :
Miss HELEN KIRK, of Glasgow,
Mr ALFRED WROE, of Manchester,
Mr JAMES WOOD (Cornet.)
ORGAN ....Mr BAKER.
LEADER OF THE BAND...........Mr JUSTICE, Jun.
CONDUCTOR ....Mr LATTER.

PROGRAMME.
PART FIRST.
OVERTURE......................" Norma " ....Bellini
                    BAND.
SONG.. ...." Rage thou angry Storm" ....Benedict
                MR ALFRED WROE.
CHORUS......................"Gipsy Chorus" ....Weber
                CHORAL UNION.
SONG........................"Spirit Song" (by desire) ....Haydn
                MISS HELEN KIRK.
AIR (with variations).................................Haydn
            ORGAN—MR BAKER.

MUSIC HALL, ABERDEEN.

Messrs HARRISON'S
SUBSCRIPTION CONCERTS
(1892-1893).
UNDER THE DISTINGUISHED PATRONAGE
OF
HER ROYAL HIGHNESS PRINCESS BEATRICE,
PRINCESS HENRY OF BATTENBERG.

HIS ROYAL HIGHNESS PRINCE HENRY OF
BATTENBERG, K.G.

ARTISTES—
Madame ADELINA PATTI.
MISS MARGARET MACINTYRE.
MADAME AMY SHERWIN.
MDLLE. ANTOINETTE TREBELLI.
MADAME ANTOINETTE STERLING.
MADAME ALICE GOMEZ.
MR BEN DAVIES.

150years

Concerts

Concerts are the life blood of The Music Hall. The earliest tended to favour classical orchestral pieces with guest players and singers. The Aberdeen Philharmonic Society held its first public performance on 18th February, 1878, and although that first audience was small, the society went on to achieve popular support. From the Harrison Concert series in the 1890s through to the present evenings with The Royal Scottish National Orchestra, classical music of the highest standard has been enjoyed in the excellent acoustic environment of the concert hall.

Moura Lympany performed with The London Philharmonic, Sir John Barbirolli conducted the Halle Orchestra and Hugo Rignold the Liverpool Philharmonic, while Sir Adrian Boult, Karl Rankl and Alexander Gibson have conducted the Scottish National Orchestra.

Concerts, however, can encompass all tastes. Those held to raise funds for good causes or to entertain the 'working classes' tended to be broader in their choice of programme. Many featured Scottish music, players and comedians. The New Year Festival in aid of the Aberdeen Temperance Society is a typical example although the question has to be asked - did Mr Harry Lauder, comedian, have the nerve to sing *Just a Wee Doch an Doris Afore Ye Gang Awa*?

Mr Harry Lauder, comedian

MUSIC HALL, ABERDEEN.
GRAND
EVENING CONCERT,
28th FEBRUARY, 1878.
COMMENCE AT EIGHT O'CLOCK.
GALLERY, FRONT ROW, SOFA STALLS.
ROW No. 2
SIX SHILLINGS.
ENTRANCE FROM SILVER STREET.

ABERDEEN TEMPERANCE SOCIETY'S
GREAT NEW-YEAR
FESTIVAL,
MUSIC HALL
SATURDAY, 1st JANUARY, 1898.
ARTISTES :—
Mr HARRY LAUDER, Comedian.
Miss FLORA DONALDSON, Soprano.
Mr BALLARD BROWNE, Baritone.
Miss JUANITA JONES, The Welsh Contralto.
THE ROYAL QUINTETTE, Dancers.
THE STAR QUARTETTE, Instrumentalists.
Mr J. M. HAMILTON
The "Scottish Sims Reeves."
Miss JOHNSTONE PETRIE, Scotch Reader.
Mr DOVE PATERSON, Elocutionist.
Madame BURRELLI, the Lady Whistler.
Mr WILL PENDER Bell Performer.
Mr MANSON SKINNER, Dance Artiste.
Mr SCOTT-SKINNER the "Strathspey King."
GORDON's COLLEGE TEAM, Vaulting Exhibition.
Mr J. R. BROOKE, Organist and Pianist.

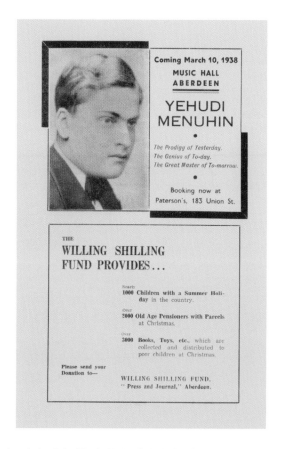

The 1938 Willing Shilling Fund was an early example of the support given to local charities by the North East's leading newspaper. It provided a summer holiday in the country for nearly 1000 children, Christmas parcels for over 2000 old-age pensioners and over 3000 books and toys for poor children at Christmas.

A Variety
of Concerts

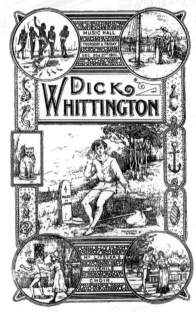

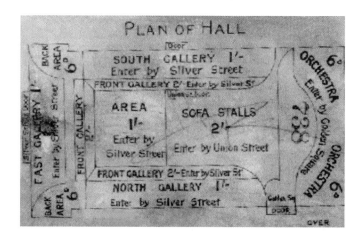

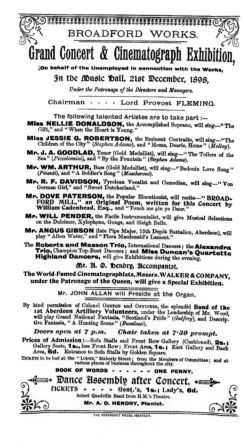

On the reverse of the ticket from 1892 (above) for the Second Annual Grand Highland Concert is a plan of The Music Hall showing the seating arrangements, the prices and how to gain access to each area. The most expensive seats appear to be the Sofa Seats, which are closest to the platform. These appear to be similar to the 'fauteuils', which can be found in older theatres. They are double-upholstered seats, like small sofas.

Cinema

The Music Hall had the honour of hosting Aberdeen's first public demonstration of the cinématographe. Just a mere nine months after the first showing by the Lumière brothers in Paris, 18 short films were shown on the 28th, 29th and 30th September, 1896, including one that featured hand-stencilled colour.

Before the spread of Donald's cinemas across the city, the novelty of watching moving films became an interesting attraction to bring an audience to a concert evening.

Bazaars

With its many rooms, kitchens and toilets, the Assembly Rooms, with the adjoining Music Hall, was an ideal venue for fund-raising activities.

Many of the city churches were built in the 1800s, and they needed sales of work, or bazaars as they were better known, to pay off the building costs. One outstanding bazaar was the one organised to build new outdoor curling rinks in the Parish of Dyce.

The organisers engaged the services of Mr George M. Bridges of Kings Lynn, the eminent bazaar artist. Following the theme of an Ice Carnival, he created stalls that represented homes from England, Austria, Norway, Switzerland, Iceland, Russia, Siberia, Germany and Canada. At the east end of the hall he created one of the famous Ice Palaces of Montreal, whilst on the platform he created the mighty St Lawrence River with islands, rapids, cataracts and ice-tipped mountains. He also took over one of the rooms for his own waxwork display.

At all of these bazaars, various entertainments were offered to draw in the crowds and relieve them of their pennies. There were waxworks, shooting galleries and dioramas in addition to the normal stalls. The Dyce Bazaar offered 'The Mesmeric Sailor' and 'The Wonders of Science'. The Futty Kirk offered 'The New Photography' - 'Rontgen Rays'. No problems with health and safety in 1896! There were competitions for men dressing up in ladies hats and also washing competitions for men with boxes of soap as prizes! The main attraction for one bazaar was an 'Automatic Weighing Machine' - put in a penny and it printed a card with your weight - first time in Aberdeen!

FUTTIE KIRK BAZAAR BOOK

MUSIC HALL, 18TH & 19TH DECR 1896.

Grand Bazaar

FOR THE LIQUIDATION OF John Street E.U. Church Debt

· Ball Room · Music Hall Buildings ·

Friday and Saturday, 6th & 7th March, 1891.

· ADMISSION ·
Friday – 12 to 3 – 1/- after 3 p.m 6d
Saturday all day 6d

PRICE 1d

Official Guide to BAZAAR.

MUSIC HALL BUILDINGS

Friday and Saturday, 21st & 22nd October, 1904.

BEECHGROVE UNITED FREE CHURCH. ABERDEEN.

The BOOK OF THE BAZAAR

Pictures and Print.

SKENE STREET CONGREGATIONAL CHURCH. ABERDEEN.

Music Hall Buildings. Friday & Saturday. 9th & 10th October, 1903.

BOOK OF THE BAZAAR

IN THE BALL-ROOM, MUSIC HALL, ABERDEEN,

Friday & Saturday, 17th & 18th October,

IN CONNECTION WITH

St. PAUL STREET E.U. CHURCH.

Rev. A. Brown, Minister.

Opened by Dr. FARQUHARSON, M.P., on FRIDAY, 17th Oct., at ONE p.m.
Chairman, · · Lord Provost Stewart.

Opened by PETER ESSLEMONT, Esq., M.P., on SATURDAY, 18th October, at TWELVE Noon.
Chairman, · · Rev. A. Brown.

ONE PENNY.

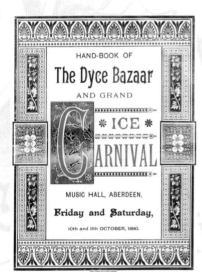

HAND-BOOK OF

The Dyce Bazaar

AND GRAND

* ICE *
CARNIVAL

MUSIC HALL, ABERDEEN,

Friday and Saturday,

10th and 11th OCTOBER, 1890.

FLOWER STALL

Under the charge of
MISS JESSIE LUNAN

GENERAL STALLS

Miss Baird
Mr Collie
Miss Dayell
Miss Douglas
Misses Duthie
Mrs Farquharson
Rev. — Farrell
Mr C. Gordon
Miss Gorbon
Mr J. Lumsden
Mr J. C. M'Kay
Mr Macdonald
Miss Milne
Mr Scroggie
Mr Thomson
Mr J. Williams

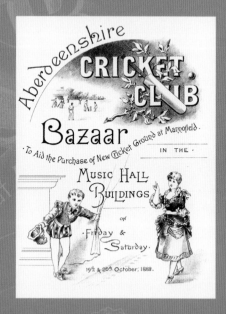

Aberdeenshire CRICKET CLUB
Bazaar
To Aid the Purchase of New Cricket Ground at Mannofield
IN THE
MUSIC HALL BUILDINGS
on
Friday & Saturday
19th & 20th October, 1888.

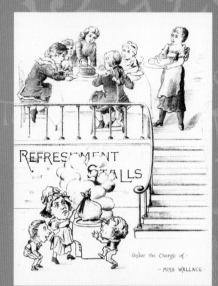

REFRESHMENT STALLS

Under the Charge of
MISS WALLACE

Game Stall

Under the Charge of
W KENDALL BURNETT, ESQ
and
CAPT MICHELL

What a remarkable contribution the ladies made to raising funds for the new cricket pitch at Mannofield

However the men were 'Game'

Adverts

Every bazaar had its brochure giving the programme of events and entertainment for that particular bazaar. These brochures are an interesting piece of social history. The advertisements in them reveal the types of businesses in Aberdeen at the time, which were supporting these fund-raising activities.

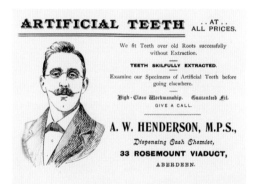

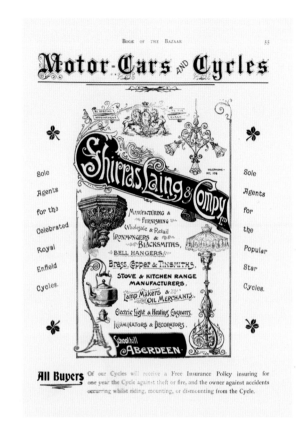

The Barefoot Queen

After Queen Victoria's popular visit to Aberdeen on 13th October, 1863, the City Fathers decided that a statue should be erected in her honour.

The commission went to sculptor Alexander Brodie (1830 - 1867), and he was asked to prepare a full-size model in plaster for approval by Her Majesty and Aberdeen Town Council.

Sittings were arranged at Balmoral Castle. When shown a photograph of the model, Queen Victoria asked that the final marble statue should show her wearing a Scottish plaid instead of a court dress. Her Royal Highness duly prepared a pen-and-ink sketch of what she thought would be appropriate. The original plaster model now stands in the foyer of The Music Hall. The town council had reservations about the portrayal of Her Majesty showing a bare foot. Her modesty was restored in the final marble statue by encasing her foot in a shoe.

That statue was placed at the corner of St Nicholas Street and Union Street, where the entrance to Marks and Spencers now stands, and unveiled by The Prince of Wales in March, 1866. Within a few years, it was damaged by weather conditions. To save it from further deterioration, it was moved in 1887 to its present position in the entrance hall to the City Chambers.

The 'shocking' bare foot

Modesty restored with a shoe

MUSIC HALL

The Strachan Murals

Along the walls of The Music Hall are panels containing a suite of murals by the artist Robert Douglas Strachan who was born in Aberdeen in 1875. He was also responsible for the large mural on the theme of 'Apollo and The Muse's in the apse behind the organ. This replaced an earlier scheme on the same theme painted by Messrs Purdie, Bonnar and Carfrae, who were responsible for the decoration of the principal rooms of The Music Hall in 1863 - 1865.

The wall panel murals are on an Orpheus theme and depict various episodes from the Orpheus and Eurydice classical legend. Strachan started work on them in 1899 and continued for eight to ten years.

The paintings are in the mainstream of European Art Nouveau and remind us of the close links between Scottish art and the continent. They are the only surviving examples of the artist's early decorative work. He painted the panels on large canvases in his studio, and they were then glued on to the plaster walls.

Sadly, over the ensuing years, these panels deteriorated. At some time it was felt that their appearance was so bad that a decision was taken to paint over them with standard decorator's materials. Four panels were restored in 1991, but attempts to soften the overpainting with solvents in the other panels also damaged Strachan's original work.

Fortunately, some of the panels had been varnished, which gave a dividing layer and it was found that the overpainting could be removed by mechanical means. A conservation and restoration programme began in 1995.

*This large mural sits at the back of the balcony and depicts
Orpheus seated in a long sailing boat*

The panel on the left side of the stage was painted by Hugh Adam Crawford, head of Gray's School of Art, and was presumably to replace a Strachan panel that had been damaged. It was completed in 1949.

Robert Douglas Strachan's later work in stained glass is renowned, with examples in King's College, Aberdeen, the New College and the Scottish National War Memorial in Edinburgh. His work for the Goldsmith's Window in St Paul's Cathedral was destroyed during the London Blitz of 1940 - 1941. Strachan also produced windows for Britain's contribution to The Peace Palace in The Hague in the Netherlands.

Hugh Adam Crawford's panel

The panel on the left-hand wall was the centre piece of an extensive and complex conservation rescue. That was first mooted in 1986 when, with the support of the Department of Historic Buildings and Monuments (now known as Historic Scotland), the restoration of the Strachan panels was undertaken. Its poor state necessitated its removal in 1995, and it was stored at South Gyle Studio in Edinburgh. Before removing it from the wall, it was given a paper-facing layer to protect the paint surface from damage. The removal was a slow process. The painting was suspended on a cradle as the adhesive layer between the canvas and the plaster wall was manually separated.

*The restored panel was rehung in situ
in August 2004*

At the studio, the back of the canvas was cleaned very slowly using thixotropic gels and then stretched on a loom to allow it to return to its original shape. It was then lined with a support fabric. Only then could restoration and retouching be undertaken using egg tempera and dammar resin mediums.

Choirs

With its wonderful acoustics, The Music Hall provided an ideal performance platform for choirs. Concerts and competitions for school children were well supported and, along with performances by local adult choirs, they were slotted into a varied programme of professional singers and singing groups from across the world.

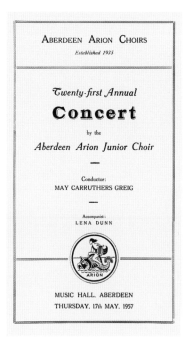

Ashley Road School Choir winning in 1952 or 1953

Girls waiting outside The Music Hall before competing in the Vocal Solo Class in May, 1956. The winner was Patricia MacMahon, who went on to become a professional soprano and a singing teacher at the Royal Scottish Academy of Music and Drama.

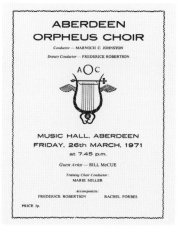

The photograph above shows the full complement of the Aberdeen Arion Choir with their indomitable conductor, May Carruthers Greig, on stage at The Music Hall in 1944. In the 1950s and 60s, they filled the hall for two or sometimes three nights. Mrs Greig insisted that each choir member had to sell as many tickets as possible. Since the seats were not allocated when tickets were bought, choir members had to get up very early and queue on a Saturday morning to book the best seats for their supporters. Sleepy-heads ended up with seats at the very back.

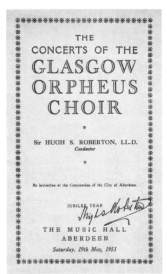

The programme for the final concert by the Glasgow Orpheus Choir in 1951 led by their famous conductor Sir Hugh S. Roberton, LLD

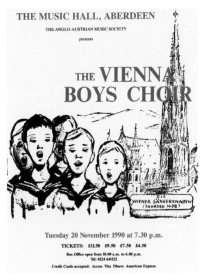

The Vienna Boys Choir were regular and popular visitors to Aberdeen

World Champion

In January, 1931, World Champion Roller Skater, Arnold Binns, from Hebden Bridge, attempted to improve on his world record at the skating rink in The Music Hall. A large crowd had gathered to watch the attempt, and they were bitterly disappointed when, after only a few hours, he retired with blistered feet.

Haydn Maxwell, the professional manager of The Music Hall Rink stepped forward and said he would attempt the record. Four minutes later, he was joined by Mr Robert Bruce, an amateur skater of 31 Rosemount Place, Aberdeen. Together they skated from early Thursday morning until just before midnight on Saturday 17th January, and established a new World Record for Non Stop Roller Skating of 61 hours 36 minutes.

Both men, who had done no preparation beforehand, agreed to skate the same length of time. Mr Maxwell finished strongly and gave a demonstration of ornamental skating until Mr Bruce, who was slightly distressed, completed his attempt. However, Mr Bruce recovered quickly and was back skating on the Monday.

During the attempt, the audience was entertained by artistes from the Tivoli Theatre and led in community singing by Mr Fred Duprez who was appearing in the farce *My Wife's Family* at His Majesty's Theatre. Amazing scenes marked the closing stages, and the skaters finished in a blaze of triumph. Such was the public interest, encouraged by daily coverage in the press, that extra police were called to regulate the crowds and many failed to gain admission.

As an amateur, Mr Bruce made no financial gain from holding the record. He was presented with a gold medal and a silver cup, which are still in the family's possession. Both he and Mr Maxwell were guests at a dinner in their honour at The Music Hall.

Robert Bruce and Haydn Maxwell

At the time of the world record attempt, Robert Bruce was 25 and employed as a stone polisher. He retired in 1973 as warehouse manager of a national cheese company and died on 19th February, 1976, aged 70.

Last Lap TO-NIGHT for the World's Endurance Skating Record. HAYDN MAXWELL and ROBERT BRUCE'S Wonderful Efforts have Captivated all Hearts. *THEY CAN JUST DO IT.* Come Along to the——

MUSIC HALL

and Cheer them during the Last Few Hours required for Victory *SKATING TO-NIGHT UNTIL MIDNIGHT.*

WILL THEY DO IT?

ROLLER SKATING TO BE BEATEN?

There is now a strong probability that the world's roller-skating endurance record will be broken to-night in Aberdeen. At 10.9 on Thursday morning Hadyn Maxwell, manager of the Music Hall Skating Rink, and W. Bruce set out in an endeavour to exceed the record of 61½ hours, held by Arnold Binns, the Yorkshire skater. To do this they have to keep on till 11.30 to-night.

Mr Robert Bruce, World Champion Non Stop Roller Skater, at his retirement presentation in 1973

The Town Council

Prior to the Great War (1914 - 1918) The Music Hall enjoyed a constant succession of concerts, bazaars, religious and political meetings and was seldom empty. The after effect of that carnage and the advent of the Jazz Age changed the public's interest and taste. The shareholders of the Aberdeen Music Hall Company faced diminishing returns and, by 1928, it was in the hands of the liquidators with instructions to offer the buildings and its contents to Aberdeen Town Council.

An initial offer of £27,250 by the council was rejected and on 15th May, 1928, a figure of £34,000 was agreed 'for behoof of the Common Good'.

During the next few decades, The Music Hall continued to act as a focal point for various functions and activities. Trade exhibitions, wrestling matches and variety concerts, with popular big-name bands, proved popular. However, the wear and tear on the building was beginning to show. One press critic of a wonderful concert by the great singer Paul Robeson noted that 'it was disgraceful that the interval should be spent in a cold, dismal, stone floored back entrance hall, without even a biscuit or a cup of coffee to buy'.

During the 1960s, the city of Aberdeen underwent expansion and re-development, and many felt The Music Hall was in urgent need of total reconstruction to meet the then-current demands for functions and conferences, or even demolition!

The Edinburgh-based Real Estate Company offered to buy The Music Hall to demolish and rebuild as part of a large development scheme for Union Street. A public outcry ensued. Ian Fleming, the head of Gray's School of Art, led the local protest.

Paul Robeson

Giant development scheme for shops and offices in Murrayfield's new bid

'SCRAP THE MUSIC HALL– IT'S A WHITE ELEPHANT'

A civic headache— planning convener

Headline from the Evening Express, 1st December 1961

150years

Nationally, Alexander Gibson, conductor of The Scottish National Orchestra, stated that the Music Hall is as good as any other concert hall not only in Britain but on the Continent. In 1965, Sir John Barbirolli protested that to demolish a hall with such wonderful acoustics would be a sacrilege of the highest order.

A very lively public debate followed. A local businessman, Mr I. Lewis Smith, managing director of the heating and refrigeration firm Spark's of Aberdeen, came up with his own design that would retain The Music Hall frontage and repeat it on the site of the former Royal Northern Club to give an elegant frontage stretching from Silver Street to Huntly Street.

In 1962, the Scottish Secretary ruled that The Music Hall would be listed as a Category A building and that his permission must be sought before the town council could proceed with any redevelopment. A public enquiry was ordered, which was held in 1973, to find a possible solution to the conflict between preserving the heritage of the building and the need to upgrade it to make it fit for modern use. It ruled that Archibald Simpson's Round and Square rooms and James Matthew's Concert Hall must be preserved.

The Round Room

The Square Room

Several options were considered over the next few years. Some redecoration was carried out from time-to-time, but it little enhanced the building. Finally, in August 1983, Aberdeen District Council's policy committee recommended complete restoration and refurbishment of The Music Hall at a cost of almost £3 million. The City Architect, Ian Ferguson, now had to seek all the necessary planning approvals and to prepare a thorough brief for this listed building. This extensive task was undertaken with complete efficiency and work started 1st October, 1984.

On 12th May, 1986, the true glory of The Music Hall was once again revealed to the public eye. The Band of the Royal Marines led a horse-drawn procession to The Music Hall. This event reflected the events of that wet and windy day in April, 1820, when the grand procession of bedecked freemasons had laid down the foundation stone of the County Assembly Rooms.

In April, 2004, The Music Hall along with its sister venue, His Majesty's Theatre and the Aberdeen Box Office, were transferred from Aberdeen City Council into the hands of Aberdeen Performing Arts, a charitable company set up specifically to run the venues. In 2008, the Lemon Tree venue became part of Aberdeen Performing Arts.

The photograph of a packed Music Hall (top right) displays the colour scheme and decoration designed by Peter Rice for the refurbishment carried out on 1986. He was also responsible for the glorious colour scheme for the restoration of His Majesty's Theatre (centre) in 1982. From its opening in 1906, HMT had always been painted white with the only colour coming from the rich red of the velvet curtains and seat coverings.

Peter's scheme of different shades of creams and soft greys highlighted by 24-carat gold decoration adds hugely to the enjoyment of a visit to this famous Matcham theatre.

The Music Hall

His Majesty's Theatre

Apollo surveys all from his lofty perch in the apse above the mighty Willis Organ

150years

Young People

The author has a vague memory from his early childhood of appearing on the stage of The Music Hall in the back of the chorus, dressed as a (Portuguese?) fisherman for a performance of *Pedro the Fisherman* by St Clement's Street School Playcentre. The star of the show was Drew Baxter, from Fittie, playing the lead part, and he had a great singing voice.

The hall was a popular venue for appearances by young people, especially the uniformed organisations. For many years, the Aberdeen Battalion of the Boys' Brigade held their gymkhana and Founder's Day parades in the building. The gymkhana featured turns by companies from the city and '12-mile roon'. Most acts featured the work of the Boys' Brigade - groundwork, horse and parallel bars, marching and general PE. Some companies entertained with hilarious comedy items.

The highlight was always the final of the exercise competition, competing for the Glentanar Shield.

Lt Barney Marshall leads in the Colour Party at the Founder's Day Parade under the watchful eye of Bandmaster Cormack Watt

18th Company BB with the Glentanar Shield, which they won in 1949 with Capt Archie Speirs, Lt Matt Rennie and pianist Joey Robb

MUSIC HALL

The sister organisation, the Girls Guildry, also presented shows depicting their activities.

In 1946, The Music Hall and the Girl Guides were honoured by a Royal visit. HRH Princess Elizabeth was welcomed to the city by Aberdeen's then best-known citizen, Lord Provost Thomas Mitchell, who served the city throughout the Second World War. Her Royal Highness saluted the march past of all sections of the organisation.

After addressing the packed auditorium, Princess Elizabeth departed through a guard of honour of Sea Rangers with a wave to the crowds lining Union Street.

On 9th October, 1930, the Girl Guides transformed
The Music Hall to create a spectacular outdoor
scenario for their fund-raising bazaar

Wrestling & other sports

From the 1930s, the art of wrestling drew crowds every second Tuesday to The Music Hall. It was not regarded as cultural entertainment, and indeed many critics felt it lowered the whole tone of what was intended to be Aberdeen's premier concert hall. However, it was a major source of income for a venue that was struggling to survive financially. The main promoter was the long-established firm of Relwyskow and Green of Leeds. In 1976, they failed to agree the increased rent imposed by the council and hosted their last match in September of that year. An attempt was made to revive the attraction the following year but it was short-lived.

Many of the stars of the then-popular Saturday afternoon coverage on television appeared on The Music Hall stage. Legend has it, that after knocking the living daylights out of each other in the ring, the contestants were known to retire, after the show, to the Grill Bar across Union Street from The Music Hall to toast each other's good health. Contrary to rumour, there appears to be no truth in the claim that the wrestlers rehearsed their contests every afternoon!

Other sports using The Music Hall included boxing, table tennis, badminton and basketball. A Sportsman of the Year presentation was a regular feature throughout the 1950s.

Jackie Pallo was always a great favourite with the ladies

Councillor Scott Sutherland presents the Basketball Cup to the Aberdeen Thistle Team, winners in March 1958. The team included Bill Williamson, Bob Duncan, Harry Lawson, Ian Shaw, Eric Auld, Bill Baxter and Dennis Lee.

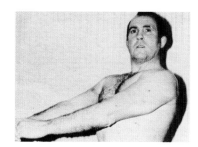

Hardman Mick McManus never failed to fire up the crowd with his often dubious tactics

Where to get your new Ration Book

CITY OF ABERDEEN (NES 2)

MINISTRY OF FOOD

CITY OF ABERDEEN FOOD OFFICE

THE ISSUE OF RATION BOOKS TO THE PUBLIC

WILL TAKE PLACE AT THE

MUSIC HALL (entrance Union Street)

FROM

APRIL 10-29, 1950

CLOSED MONDAY, APRIL 17th (Aberdeen Spring Holiday)

HOURS OF ISSUE:

MONDAY to FRIDAY (inclusive) 9.30 a.m. to 5 p.m.

SATURDAY - - 9.30 a.m. to 12.30 p.m.

The Public are requested to make application in the following
Alphabetical Order as far as possible:

WHERE THE SURNAME BEGINS WITH THE LETTER:

MONDAYS - A & B THURSDAYS M to O

TUESDAYS - C to F FRIDAYS - - P to S

WEDNESDAYS G to L SATURDAYS T to Z

People attending on their proper day may collect documents for others,
irrespective of the initial of the surname.

WHAT TO DO

1 Fill up page 4 of your present ration book and leave it in the book.
2 Then, take your ration book and identity card to the DISTRIBUTION CENTRE.

IF your identity card does not bear your right address, is lost, torn or in very bad condition, go to the FOOD OFFICE instead.

3 If you have a form RG 48 or 48E (for special rations) in your book go to the DISTRIBUTION CENTRE *unless* you need to produce a NEW medical or employers certificate, in which case go to the FOOD OFFICE instead.

4 If you hold a *temporary* identity card due for renewal at the FOOD OFFICE before 21st May, you can get your new book at the same time.

5 Persons over 70 receiving extra tea will get new tea coupons with their new books.

"Food Facts" tells you what to do after you get your new Ration Book

MINISTRY **MF** OF FOOD

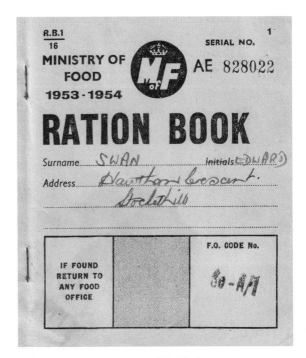

R.B.1
16

MINISTRY OF FOOD

1953-1954

SERIAL NO.

AE 828022

1

RATION BOOK

Surname *SWAN* Initials *EDWARD*

Address *Nawton Crescant.*

Gidlehill

IF FOUND RETURN TO ANY FOOD OFFICE

F.O. CODE No.

80-AA

Readers of a certain age will recall that food rationing continued for some years after the end of the Second World War in 1945

Shows and Exhibitions

From its earliest days, the large and open floor space of The Music Hall was ideally suited for trade, leisure and industrial exhibitions. Flower, cat and dog and even budgie and pigeon shows all graced the floor of the hall. During the 1950s, the Annual Ideal Homes and Trades Exhibitions were very popular and brought to the general public's attention the very latest up-to-date ideas for home modernisation.

Stands introduced the sensation of applying paint with a roller instead of a brush, string vests that were cool in summer and warm in winter and the 'Zig-Zag' skirt holder that could keep four skirts in perfect order. Entertainment was supplied by top stars from radio, television and records including the Tanner Sisters and the unique Pinky and Perky.

The Royal Horticultural Society of Aberdeen held their annual general meetings in The Music Hall from 1896 until 1926, when they moved to Shepherd's Hall in Union Terrace. They held their exhibitions in the Winter Gardens, Duthie Park, but The Music Hall was still bedecked with wonderful displays by individual flower societies.

A friend of the author submitted a bowl of dwarf tulips to the Aberdeen Rock Garden Show - it was the first time these had been shown, and his was the only entry. For his pains he was awarded second prize!

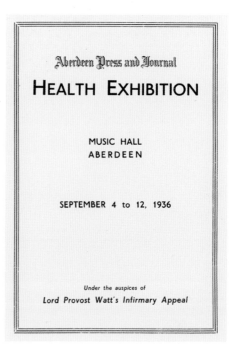

Health exhibitions in the 1930s were an important feature of health education for the citizens

A very young Eric Auld and his sister Roxelle study models at the Exhibition of Wartime Hobbies organised by the War Comfort Fund

During the Second World War, the pillared portico of The Music Hall was used as a giant advertising hoarding. This photograph shows an effort to raise £3 million to fund 60 Sunderland Flying Boats. The artwork was created by the commercial art firm Taylor & Ogston. The fund raising was supported by a march past of RAF personnel.

*The Music Hall is transformed for the Centenary Exhibition
of the Northern Co-operative Society*

Freedom Ceremonies

The Freedom of the City is the highest honour that the City of Aberdeen can bestow. It is conferred in a ceremony of ancient origin. In 12th-century Scotland, it was the means by which King David sought to bring order and prosperity to a wild and divided land.

The King's support for the formation of burghs permitted to hold fairs and weekly markets led to the creation of 'burgesses' who were merchants or craftsmen and who had the sole right to trade or manufacture. These gave them great privileges but, 'in return' they had to live in the town, pay their taxes, provide arms for the defence of the town and swear fealty to the monarch.

In later years, the awards became more selective, being made 'in token of the most devoted love and affection and of the most distinguished respect'.

Almost all ceremonies were held in The Music Hall, and from the first conferred on Lord Russell in 1859, the roll of honour lists the Prime Ministers of Australia in 1918, Canada and Australia again in 1937 and New Zealand in 1941. Field Marshall Smuts from South Africa was honoured in 1942, wartime Prime Minister Winston Churchill in 1946 with his successor, The Hon Earl Attlee, gaining his 'Burgess ticket' in 1956. Her Majesty Queen Elizabeth, the Queen Mother, received her Freedom in 1959.

In more recent times, Freedoms were granted to the outstanding political figures of Nelson Mandela in 1984 and Mikhail Gorbachev in 1993. Football manager, Alex Ferguson, the Hero of Gothenburg, was a popular Freeman in 1999.

The most recent Freedom was that granted to the comedy team, Scotland The What?, and that, most appropriately, was held in His Majesty's Theatre.

Winston and Clementine Churchill walk up Union Street after receiving the Freedom in 1946. Note the ceremonial Burgess ticket tied to Winston's hat.

Dr Mary Esslemont accepts a silver casket from Lord Provost Alec Collie, who was to receive his own Freedom in 1995. Dr Esslemont received the Freedom of the City of Aberdeen in 1981 for her lifetime of work to improve the healthcare and living conditions of Aberdeen folk.

Mikhail Gorbachev

The Ballroom

Although The Music Hall's Ballroom disappeared during the renovations of 1984 - 1986, it was, for many years, prior to the creation of the Aberdeen Arts Centre, the home for performances by very talented amateur dramatic theatre groups.

Until 1949, the Aberdeen Repertory Theatre performed regularly on the ballroom stage and at the open-air theatre at Hazlehead.

The Carden Arts Group continued to bring top-quality performances throughout the 1950s, with Ronald Jean's *Count Your Blessings*, Emlyn Williams's *Someone Waiting*, Terence Rattigan's *The Browning Version* and George Bernard Shaw's *Man of Destiny*. The December 1954 performance of *Here We Go Gathering* featured the debut in Aberdeen of Victor Carin, who had been associated for many years with the Stonehaven Dramatic Club.

A performance of *Rookery Nook* in November 1949 began what is affectionately referred to as the Bill Gavin era. William Gavin began his career in the 1930s with the Play Goers - the oldest drama group in Aberdeen. A consummate professional, he put together the finest group of amateur actors to present almost 60 shows at the Music Hall until moving to the Aberdeen Arts Centre where they presented, on 16th June, 1976, their 100th and final show *When We Are Married*.

Regulars with the William Gavin Players included Tom Alexander, Jabez Bruce, Jane Cowan, George Cusiter, Dorothy Eddie, Margaret Gill, Margaret Gray, Judy Kelly, Sheila Law, May McDonald, James McKay, John McRobb, Alistair Selway and George Sellar. Later, younger, additions to the cast lists included Jim Couper, Douglas Kynoch and Gillian Wright.

Shadow and Substance featured fine performances by well-known local actors Irene Galloway, Sheila Law, Ronald Craig, Alistair Selway and William Gavin

William Gavin

150 years

Amateur companies in Aberdeen seem to spend their lives looking for premises, rehearsal space, somewhere to store scenery and costumes, somewhere to build and paint scenery. Originally the Gavin Players rehearsed in a private house. They then moved to the old Riverside Tea Room on the banks of the River Dee before finding attic rooms in the harbour area, which served the company for 18 years. The lease was terminated in 1972 and the company was on the brink of disbanding until rehearsal facilities were provided by Aberdeen University.

The William Gavin Players not only presented the whole spectrum of dramatic art - period plays, comedies, romances and heavy dramas - they were also very active competing at drama festivals. Members of the cast were regularly engaged for plays on BBC Radio.

Many companies in Aberdeen were grateful for scenery and lighting equipment from Leo Small from his tiny shed in East North Street

After 18 years with his own company, William Gavin decided to leave Aberdeen in 1967 to join Perth Repertory Company. However the William Gavin Players continued under that title until their final 100th Show.

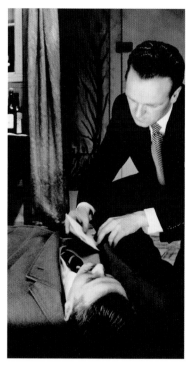

William Gavin receives his farewell gift from George Sellar, watched by members of the William Gavin Players

George Cusiter and Jabez Bruce in Dial M for Murder

The Music Hall Today

After the major refurbishment of 1984 - 1986, The Music Hall took on a fresh new life. It was farewell to the cold and depressing days of milk crates and broken chairs stacked in the entrance corridors. It was also goodbye to the days of painting scenery in the entrance foyer - as the author did in the days of the Aberdeen Revue Group!

Now for audiences, a more comfortable and welcoming environment with new toilet facilities, the new Doric Bar and Round Room Cafe and a stunning and exciting colour scheme with wonderful stencil designs created by Peter Rice. Backstage, the dressing rooms were redesigned and refurbished to elegant standards, and state-of-the-art lighting and sound equipment were installed. Booking facilities for venues across the city were centralised with the establishment of Aberdeen Box Office in the former West Room.

Things moved forward again when control was transferred in 2004 along with His Majesty's Theatre and the Box Office from Aberdeen City Council to Aberdeen Performing Arts. Since then, The Music Hall has gone from strength to strength with ever bigger names entertaining sell-out audiences.

Scanning through the publicity booklets for the last 20 years, one realises that the very best of national and international entertainment has graced the large stage at The Music Hall. The original concept and vision for the hall - culture for all tastes at affordable prices - has been amply fulfilled.

In the 1990s, classical tastes were catered for by visits from the BBC Scottish Symphony Orchestra, the London Symphony Orchestra, the Scottish Chamber Orchestra, the Royal Scottish National Orchestra, James Galway, Nigel Kennedy, Evelyn Glennie and Aberdeen Sinfonietta to pick out but a few. Broader tastes were covered by The Scottish Fiddle Orchestra, Ladysmith Black Mambazo, Eartha Kitt, Acker Bilk, Humphrey Lyttelton, The Roy Wood Spectacular, Deacon Blue, Elkie Brooks, Eddi Reader, Wolfstone, Barbara Dickson, Sidney Devine, Van Morrison and The Manic Street Preachers.

Tastes in comedy ranged across all forms of stand-up, including Lee Hurst, Fred McAulay, Lee Evans, Frank Skinner, Rob Newman, David Baddiel, Billy Connolly and Jack Dee along with the broadest humour in the words of Kevin 'Bloody' Wilson and Roy 'Chubby' Brown. Into this wonderful mixing bowl of entertainment went The Aberdeen Alternative Festival, Christmas carol concerts, Marie Curie Cancer Care concerts, charity sales, the annual performances of Handel's *Messiah* by the Aberdeen Choral Society, music and dancing festivals, fashion shows and craft fairs - plenty choice for everyone!

Many of these made repeat visits in the new century. Rock concerts were very popular with notable visits by Simple Minds, Status Quo and Bill Wyman and The Rhythm Kings.

A popular innovation was Look Who's Talking - a series of lunchtime talks by speakers from all walks of life. First to set the ball rolling was Jack Webster, others have included Roy Hattersley, Johnny Beattie, Magnus Magnusson, Sandi Toksvig, Edwina Currie, Dorothy Paul, Timothy West, John Sergeant, Tony Benn and John Simpson.

Look Who's Talking...

During the Mozart 250 Celebrations held in 2006, the Scottish Chamber Orchestra, conducted by Alexander Janiczek, presented a series of concerts featuring the composer's work including *Piano Concertos* and *Requiem*.

More recent concerts in the twenty-first century have included Strictly Strauss, Circus of Horrors, University of Aberdeen Choral Society and Orchestra, Paul Merton's Silent Clowns, Prague Symphony Orchestra, along with regular visitors the Royal Scottish National Orchestra, Scottish Chamber Orchestra and BBC Scottish Symphony Orchestra. Comedy and popular music were covered by visits from the Scottish Fiddle Orchestra, Errol Brown, the Singing Kettle, the Sound of Musicals, Ed Byrne, Rob Brydon, the Hollies, Dave Spikey and Jimmy Carr.

Aberdeen Performing Arts, using to the full their venues at The Music Hall, His Majesty's Theatre and the Lemon Tree, are providing for the North East of Scotland the very best of high-quality entertainment.

The Aberdeen Singing Chorus lead the audience in wonderful sing-along - a splendid and colourful example of a great evening's entertainment at The Music Hall

150 years

The Future

It is good to celebrate a birthday or an anniversary. It is a time to reflect on the past. A time to celebrate successes and to think about future plans.

The sesquicentennial celebration of the Music Hall revels in the glorious, inspirational, entertaining and sometimes controversial history of this iconic building. It also presents Aberdeen Performing Arts (APA) with a challenge. The challenge of extending the vision of its founding fathers that the building should be at the heart of the cultural growth of the city.

APA has commissioned a feasibility study to consider the Music Hall's future and from it a plan has been formulated to establish the Hall as a flagship centre for music in the North East – a regional centre of excellence in music, enhancing its impact on culture and tourism in the North East of Scotland.

Duncan Hendry, Chief Executive of the Trust, explains that this plan will create in the city centre a place where children will make music alongside music students, professional composers and national orchestras. It will be a vibrant venue alive with music all day.

The realisation of this vision will take time but a start has been made. An upgrade of the stalls seating and a refurbishment of parts of the auditorium is already under way. It is a small but positive investment in guaranteeing the cultural future of this popular venue.

Aberdeen Performing Arts staff take the stage in June 2009